Hello my name is Chuck Crenshaw I am the Author for the children's book Jim Bob. This is my first title to Publish and Market. This is one of many Jim Bob Stories, this is a series of books for Jim Bob. I am also writing other titles as well so be looking for those books. I am going to be Publishing other authors books as well, so watch for N House Production and Recording and stay up to date with the changes in our Titles that we offer on the Market.

For those of you that don't know me, let me introduce myself.

I am a father of 5 children that I love dearly, and a beautiful wife that loves' me. And I serve our Lord with all my heart and soul. I am a miracle within myself. And I thank the Lord for all he has done for me and my family. Helping us with all we have gone through and continuing to provide the strengths and the ability to do.

It all started with neglect to take care of myself, I broke my neck several years ago. And I neglected to really do anything about the healing at all but this is going to be another book totally about the neck.

Hopefully soon to release. But God kept me from being paralyzed permanently to being disabled with lack of feelings and weakness. I was diagnosed with Sever Cervical Stenosis. And with love and Prayers through friends and family and 2 major surgeries and almost 2 years later. I am able to bring to you readers a book of Jim Bob that I pray you will love. Jim Bob's character is a well - mannered little boy.

And it will educate little ears to be as well, he is as far country as you can go to grow up. In a fictional town called, Backwoods, Texas.

So please enjoy the Jim Bob stories now and to come and thanks from everybody that's involved with the making of Jim Bob.

Introduction: Jim Bob is a fictional character

written by and copyrighted by: Chuck Crenshaw

You will learn more about Jim Bob as the stories are being told so don't miss any of the Jim Bob Books.

His Character goes far beyond an average kid, but hopefully will inspire several young children living in today's society. This book is designed to entertain children of all ages. And please give me your feedback and your thoughts and Prayers for the making of Jim Bob

Email: to

Nhouseprodandrecording@gmail.com

Oh' no, it's almost   Thanksgiving in Backwoods, Texas said Thomas the scared Turkey, Mr. Chuck can you please write about something else cause I am too scared to read this book.

(Chuck)

Aww' Thomas;

It will be fine this is a fictional story, nobody in this book except for me, is real. So quit your worrying and enjoy the book!

(Thomas)

Are you sure Mr. Chuck, well ok then.

(Chuck)

Yes' I'm sure so come on let's go grab some popcorn and Enjoy the book!

(Thomas)

But I don't eat popcorn! How about just corn?

(Chuck)

Ok' you get corn and I will get popcorn.

(Chuck)

Uh' Thomas you think you can pay I forgot my money at home!!!

Jim Bob, he was raised on a farm in Backwoods, Texas.

Now Jim Bob loves all his friends and family, every holiday seasons they all gathered for a great big ole' feast. And Jim Bob is well known in these parts for his manners and respect for others.

Jim Bob is nearly a teenager and he is a fine Christian young man. He attends to his Community Baptist Church where he was raised. His father is great man that taught Jim Bob the joys of helping and being a Christian. And the rewards were well worth more than anything money could buy. He is a top notch student in his school and he is a 4-h member. Dedicated to volunteering his time.

   Well here it is early November folks are getting ready for their Thanksgiving cooking festival one of everybody's all, time favorite season.

And believe me you can definitely see the meaning everybody's favorite seasons.

   Well this year is going to be different than any years that

 Jim Bob has ever seen,

Please follow the Jim Bob Stories to keep up with Jim Bob

Characters listed in book 1 series are as follows

Thomas The Scared Turkey

Jim Bob

Mr. Jennings Jim Bob's dad

Scotty

Gregory

Officer Smith on a horse

Officer Toby in the Police car

Dr. Best MD

God

Jesus Christ

Dr. Roy Davis Pastor at North Shreve. Baptist Church in Shreveport, La.

My Wife, Dot Crenshaw

This is a list of every named mentioned in the book

The Fishing Trip

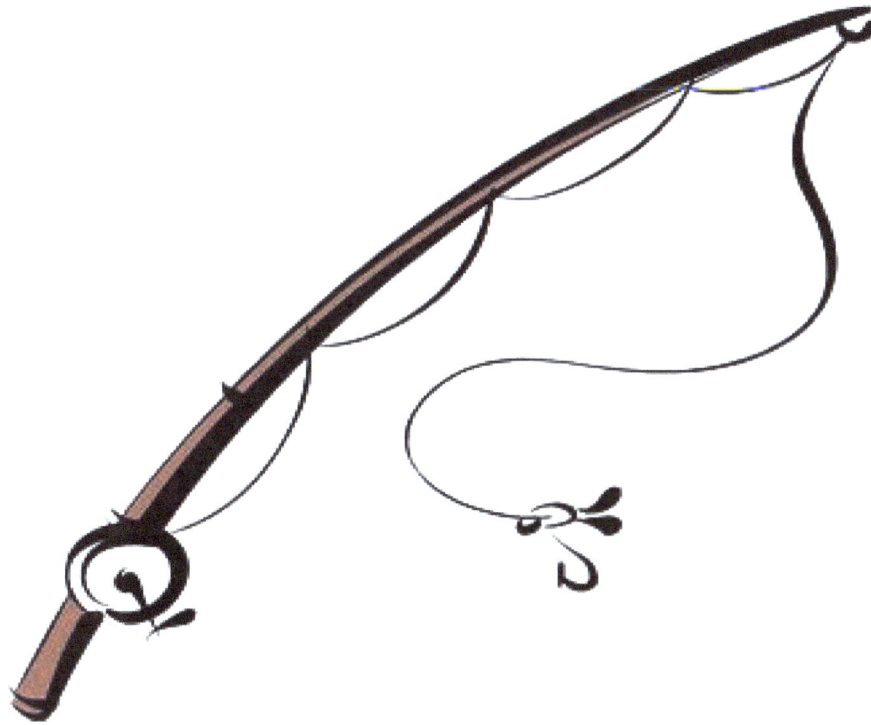

Well it's a Saturday morning, Jim Bob and his friends have been waiting for this weekend it seemed like forever.

But at last it's finally here!! The camping, fishing and hiking trip that Jim Bob's dad had promised him and his friends.

They were super excited to be going on this trip to "Camp Dreamland"

Jim Bob was up early packing his bags for the trip, he heard his dad say,

Alright boys it's nearly 5:00 a.m. time to get moving.

We got a long trip ahead of us!

Yes' sir shouted Scotty, one of Jim Bob's friends.

Don't forget your tooth brush Jim Bob shouted, because you can't use mine laughed Jim Bob'.

How far is it to Camp Dreamland Mr. Jennings asked Gregory, the other friend of Jim Bob's.

Oh' I figured about an hour and a half drive said Mr. Jennings.

So let's get the trusty rusty wagon loaded up said Mr. Jennings.

That's what they called their station wagon automobile (The Trusty Rusty Wagon)! It's ok in the country to name your cars. Just don't talk to them that would definitely look bad.

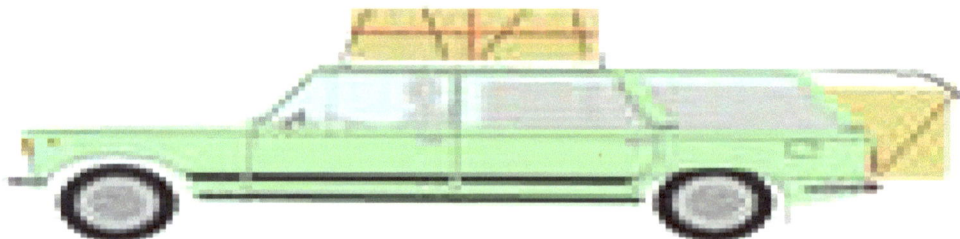

Mr. Jennings' shouted off we go!!

And sure as time was ticking they pulled into Camp Dreamland at exactly an hour and a half later.

We are here boys, now I can show you how the pro. Fishermen fish.

laughed Mr. Jennings, as he tugged on his collar of his shirt.

Now let's get the bags unloaded, while I go check us in!

Yes' sir said Gregory!

I will get your stuff Mr. Jennings said Scotty.

Well thanks Scotty' said Mr. Jennings.

We will all get his stuff said Jim Bob!

Ok settled, said Scotty we will all get his stuff.

So the boy's got the luggage unloaded, while Mr. Jennings checked them in at Camp Dreamland!!!!

Nothing seemed to be more fun than a weekend at a camp with my favorite hang-out buddy's thought Jim Bob.

So after they unpacked and got their things squared away!

Mr. Jennings says whose up to some good breakfast?

They all felt like they could do some serious eating.

Yes' me said, Gregory!

I thought you'd never ask' said Scotty!

Jim Bob, said' you don't have to ask me twice!

Well let's go to the restaurant, said Mr. Jennings, but we got to be snappy,

we are burning daylight!

So off they went to eat some great breakfast!

Thank the Lord we have great food restaurant, said Jim Bob.

Yes' indeed, chuckled Mr. Jennings.

Now who is ready to do some fine fishing against the ole Pro. laughed Mr. Jennings.

Well' said Scotty, let the battles begin.

May the best fisherman win, said Gregory.

That'll be me, said Jim Bob!

We will just have to see bout that' chuckled Mr. Jennings.

So off to the lake they go to see who can fish the best.

Well the fishing battle started and nobody has caught a single fish.
Then they heard thundering in a far-away distance.

Mr. Jennings said well that about does it boys!
We should be getting ready to leave and head back to the lodge.
Before the weather hits, just as Mr. Jennings spoke it started pouring rain.

Oh my' said Mr. Jennings, that was unexpected.
Hurry boys! Shouted, Mr. Jennings.

The wind picked up real strong, the boys rushed around in the hard
downfall of the rain!

They had been fishing for about 3 hours now, and there were no signs of
storms moving in at all, till now things were getting tremendously bad
for them. No one else was even in sight.

The rain and wind kept getting stronger and stronger.

They all finally reached the ole Trusty Rusty Wagon as they called it but not before they all heard a loud thump.

They turn and seen Mr. Jennings laying on the ground with a tree limb on top of him!

Dad, screamed Jim Bob are you alright?

No, Jim Bob I am injured' please get this limb off me shouted Mr. Jennings.

The boys rushed over to Mr. Jennings, and they proceeded to pull the big limb off of him.

The wind was really strong and the rain felt like nails, but as fast as the weather came in, it also left like nothing had ever happened.

That was some strange weather said Scotty, as they lifted the limb and carried it away.

Jim Bob asked his dad, are you alright Dad?

No Jim Bob I am afraid not, I can feel my legs!

The bad weather was gone now and there was debris scattered everywhere.

What do we need to do said Jim Bob?

Stay calm, said Gregory.

First we need a plan, said Scotty.

Good idea replied, Mr. Jennings.

Dad how far is Camp Dreamland from here? Asked, Jim Bob.

Grunting as Mr. Jennings answered, about 4 miles Jim Bob.

Would you guys mind staying with Dad while I go get help? Jim Bob asked Scotty and Gregory.

Sure we will, Scotty replied.

But is that safe for you to do? asked Gregory.

Theirs is no time to waste Dad needs help, and I am going for help. Thank you Guys I will be back soon, Said Jim Bob.

Dad you hang in there I will be back I promise, Jim Bob told his dad.

We will take care of him, Gregory said.

Yea, Jim Bob don't you worry a bit, said Scotty.

Jim Bob you be careful son, I don't want anything to happen to you my son, said Mr. Jennings.

Yes' Sir replied, Jim Bob as he struck out running for help.

In search of someone to bring his dad to safety. And didn't know what he was going to find, he just knew they needed help quick for his dad.

Well it seemed like Jim Bob had been gone for hours, but he had only been gone for a short few minutes.

I sure hope Jim Bob is ok and he finds help fast, said Gregory.

I do too, said Scotty.

He will boys replied Mr. Jennings in fact he is a full fledge trooper of bravery.
In fact, you all are and I thank you boys for your help.
Now let's put this matter in God's hands and pray for every one's safety.

Mean, while back with Jim Bob and his search for help.

He had only been gone for about 45 minutes.
When he run up to a man riding a horse with a cowboy hat and some type of radio.

Jim Bob screamed out, Sir, Sir my dad.

 Jim Bob was give out from running all this time that he couldn't hardly talk.

The man said whoa! Son slow down and breath!

What seems to be your troubles? said the man.

It took a second but Jim Bob finally was able to talk.

It's my dad sir, he has been seriously injured down at the lake
A huge limb fell on him as the storm came through, explained Jim Bob.

Yea son, I know about the storm we have several downed trees and powerlines
in the area, let me radio for help, said the Officer.

Great, said Jim Bob I have help at last!

And the Officer did just that, he radioed for help in fact he ordered a medical chopper to fly out and bring Mr. Jennings to safety.

Hop on my horse with me son, I will give you a ride back to the Lake where your Dad is, I have a medical team that is going to fly out and bring him to the doctor explained the nice Officer.

Yes' Sir, said Jim Bob,

My Dad is going to get to fly? ask Jim Bob.

You bet son, said the Officer.

The chopper is in flight headed that way now, replied the Officer.

My name is Officer Smith son, what is your name?

My name is Jim Bob and thank you, sir for your kindness and help.

The Officer chuckled and said it's my pleasure oh' and it's my job and they both laughed.

And the Officer told Jim Bob now don't you worry we are going to take good care of your dad!

Jim Bob said with excitement in his voice, yes sir.

When Jim Bob and the Officer got back to the Lake the Chopper was circling around fixing to land.

Gregory shouted, look at the helicopter wow!

Scotty said, that's so cool Mr. Jennings you're going to fly.

Jim Bob hopped off the horse ran over to see his dad.

How are you, dad? asked Jim Bob.

I have been better but I am certainly glad to see your back safely replied Mr. Jennings with a weak voice!

Dad this is Officer Smith, Jim Bob to his dad.

Hello Officer Smith sir and thank you for your help, replied Mr. Jennings.

It is my pleasure, said the officer.

Now let's get you loaded up in the medical chopper and get you to the doctor shouted the Officer.

So they loaded Mr. Jennings in the chopper and the Officer radioed for a squad car to pick up the boys and carry them to the hospital to meet Mr. Jennings.

While on their way to the hospital the boys introduced themselves to the police officer. The Officer name was Toby.

Officer says to the boys, have either one of you, boy's ever rode in a police car?

No sir, they all replied.

Would you like to hear the siren? said the nice officer.

That would be awesome, said Scotty.

It would be great, said Gregory.

So the officer turned on the siren.

Oh wow, said Jim Bob.

Officer Toby, says Jim Bob.

Yes, Jim Bob, replied Officer Toby.

I thank you for your help and I think I want to be a police officer when I grow up too, said Jim Bob.

Well then you can definitely be a great policeman, said officer Toby.

And your very welcome responded officer Toby.

They arrive at the hospital and they say thank say thanks to Officer Toby.

And Officer Toby walks them in to find the Doctor.

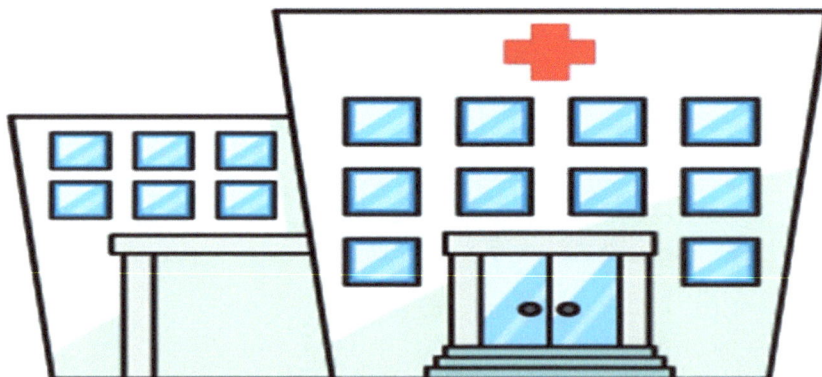

They found the Doctor that is taking care of Mr. Jennings, and he asked the boys to step into an empty room for a conversation with him he introduces his self
As Dr. Best MD.

Your dad has a bad injury to his spine although he is going to be fine he is going to be in a wheel chair for sometimes I don't know how long yet. So Jim Bob he is definitely going to need lots of help. Can you handle helping him Jim Bob, asked Dr. Best.

Oh' yes sir, said Jim Bob as long as he is going to be alright?

Dr. Best replied, I knew you could handle it and yes he is going to be fine.

Gregory said, you're not alone Jim Bob we will help too.

Scotty said, yes that's what best buds do for each other.

Thanks guys replied Jim Bob and thank you Dr. Best sir.

Dr. Best told the boys that they could go back and see Mr. Jennings now, but he didn't know how long he would be in the Hospital.

So off to the room to see Mr. Jennings.

How are you doing dad, asked Jim Bob?

Well I can't move my legs, and I can't walk for now but with God at my side leading me I am unstoppable, giggled Mr. Jennings.

Yes, sir said Jim Bob! happy to hear his dad talk like that.

And we can push your wheel chair when you need to go somewhere, said Gregory.

Yes, we can definitely get you around, smiled Scotty cause I am a race car driver Scotty told Mr. Jennings.

Ok there Mr. Race car driver, I think we need to keep you away from my wheel chair, chuckled Mr. Jennings.

Well as the days past and it was becoming Thanksgiving in Backwoods, Texas

The whole town showed up at the hospital with lots of food trays that was just unaminable. But the town folks still had their family feast just with a much bigger family. You see when God loves he don't just love sometimes he loves all the time and for every one to show up at the hospital to be with folks that couldn't go anywhere, but there! It was fantastic, the town folks fed everyone there Hospital workers, patients and their visitors. See in Backwoods Texas they believe in honesty and the word of God. And coming together as a community and helping and sharing, teaching others about our Lord and Savior Jesus Christ and sharing the word of truth The Holy Bible.

My Pastors Name at North Shreve. Baptist Church in Shreveport, La. is

 Dr.Roy Davis.

Do you Know your Pastor Name if so write his name here_____
for a special prayer for him and his entire congrigation.

If so maybe you could show him you wrote his name in Jim Bob story book.

I would imagine he would love that don't you thin? We are going to say a prayer at the end of this book write down who you prayed for and why. So when you Pray again you can pray for the specific reason of the prayer. Although you don't have to because God knows everything, so he knows each individual problem's that we Pray for.

So several days past and Mr. Jennings is still in the Hospital it's been almost 6 long weeks of hard therapy for Mr. Jennings but like the boys said they would be there to help him and they all did just that.

Have you ever help anybody with a medical problem or an ederly person

If so, write their names here _____.

The boys actually enjoyed helping Mr. Jennings, he made it fun no matter the pain he was in from his spinal injury. He knew this was going to be a tough battle to face alone so he was going to need the boys for everything.
He prayed for comfort in his pain and agony but knew that God wasn't going to put more on him than he could handle.

This was the beginning of a long journey for Mr. Jennings and all his life, long friends and neighbors. But the real meaning is no matter the struggles life has for you someone is willing to participate and help you with your struggles never give up your faith. Faith in God alone and his Love is better than any Medicine designed by man.

The love of God and his Son Jesus Christ is better to us in any ways that you could possibly imagine. So the Jim Bob stories are not to preach to you but to educate the young and maybe even touch the adults to inspire all readers to believe in the word of God.

All things are Possible through Jesus Christ our Lord and Savior!!

That's a scripture from the Bible please look it up and research the meaning and write it in this book.

And I pray someday I will meet you and you will know the meaning and want me to sign your book. I am the Author of Jim Bob and I am directly talking to you through the Love of God and our Savior Jesus Christ.

I am telling you this, because I have lived the part of being hospitalized in a wheel chair. Not knowing if I was ever going to walk again.

And I am writing my book to share with the world but for now please continue reading Jim Bob and May God Bless your every Purchase of my Books now and to come.

This book is Dedicated to Every Ear and Every Eye to enjoy and share.

This is a special prayer that the Author Chuck Crenshaw would like to pray with you!

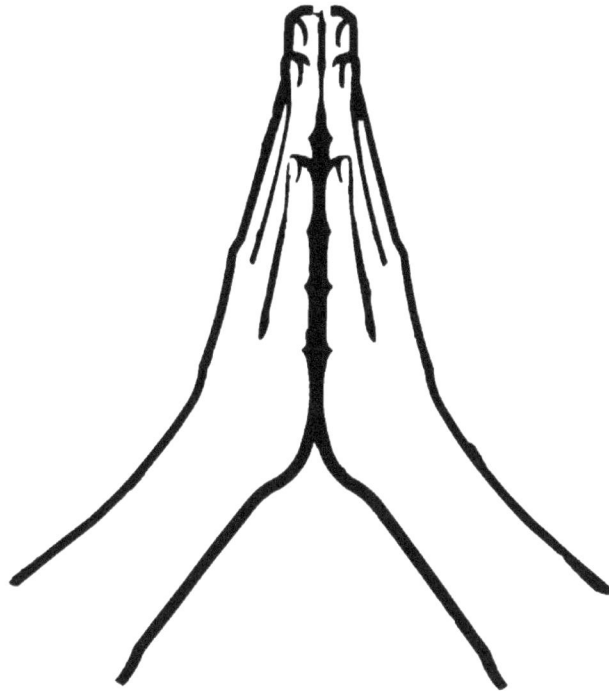

Please Pray with Me:

God above you have the control to reach everyone through my book please God even if I never know who this may touch. I pray to you, to let this book continue in your blessing, to encourage and educate the young and inspire the lost. And bring them to understand your word, I myself struggle to remain a faithful Christian, so I know the path can be threatened and sometimes short for some. But God I ask, that you use me and my Books in your Power to touch and surrender us, for your needs and let us do your will. God I also ask if you would guide my Church and all other Churches to preach your word stronger than ever and educate our lost Country to bring your word to their wisdom I love you and ask for my many sins to be forgiven and strengthen me as a Christian of strong Faith.
I pray this prayer in honor of your Sons Powerful and Holy Name
Amen…………………………………

Thanks and please continue to enjoy upcoming Jim Bob Stories

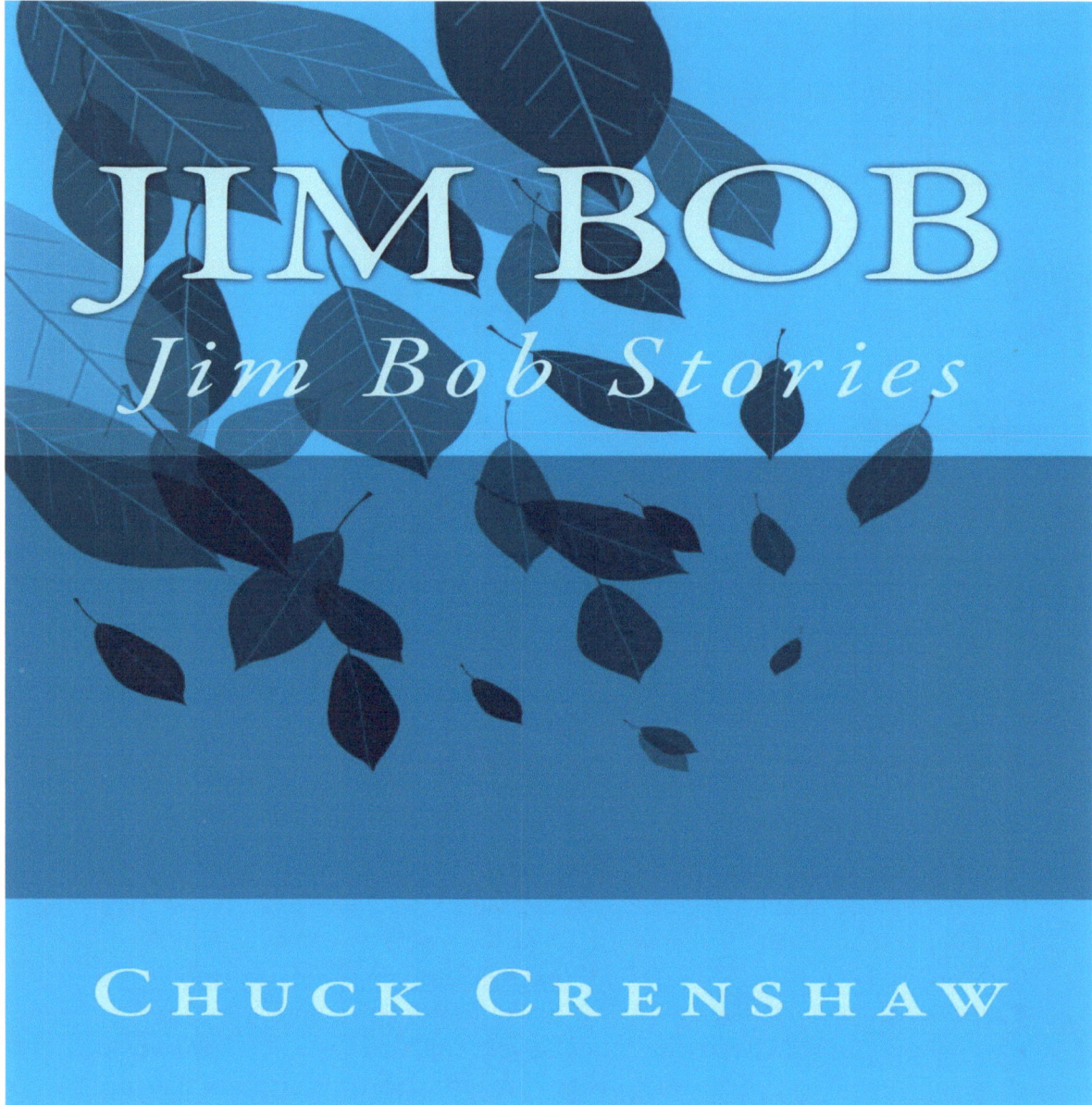

JIM BOB

Jim Bob Stories

CHUCK CRENSHAW

Jim Bob is being read all over the world your child's name and pictures or drawings can be viewed all over the world. Please state in your submission child's age, what state and possibly town they reside in no information will be used in the book except name age and state and any information provided by the legal Guardian of the participating child.

This page is left blank for your drawings or special prayer or Letter to Jim Bob.

So don't wait to submit your child's submission before the dead line which is January 31st 2016 for your child's submission for drawings, Name, and Picture for the Jim Bob stories

Drawing must be drawn by your child and signed at the bottom right of the picture of the child and legal guardian for the Author to legally use the art work in the Jim Bob Stories. Only going to submit a chosen few so please act now. Please email this submission to

JIM BOB att.

To: Nhouseprodandrecording@gmail.com.

But if for some reason you couldn't make the deadline keep posted through Jim Bob and watch for further entries in the future. Because every child deserves a little fame. At least in my eyes, and that's in Jesus' eyes too.

I want to thank my wife who has really been my support in everything I do, she has loved me endlessly through all my pains and complaints. She is a strong woman she is also a cancer survivor. And I am extremely proud of her.

Regardless of her well beings or her pains, she was there to comfort me in mine. I could say more but there's no need, it's all going to be told in my autobiography. Hopefully soon, I will be Publishing more books in the future.

So keep up with N House Production and Recording for future changes. Thank you for becoming a loyal fan of mine and all other Authors that are Published with N House Production and Recording.

Jim Bob Stories
Written by: Chuck Crenshaw
Copyrighted by: Chuck Crenshaw 2015
Published by: N House Production and Recording (owner) Dot Crenshaw
Shreveport, La.
Manufactured by: Createspace - North Charleston, South Carolina
Illustrations used by free images by public domain

North Shreve. Baptist Church where I am currently a member and love everyone there very dearly!!

Autograph Page:

Author: Chuck Crenshaw
Book series Jim Bob
N House Production and Recording: Publisher

This Page is for all autographed books for meet and greet, hopefully I will see you soon. At book signings all over, and I personally will thank you for your support on Jim Bob stories.

Author_____